COMPASS
True Stories for Kids

D1490198

L'NU'K
The People

Mi'kmaw History, Culture, and Heritage

Theresa Meuse

NIMBUS
PUBLISHING LTD

Nimbus Publishing Limited
3731 Mackintosh Street, Halifax, NS, B3K 5A5
(902) 455-4286 nimbus.ca

Printed and bound in Canada

NB1082

Main cover photo: Lynda Mallett
Inset cover photos (L–R): Theresa Meuse, iStock, Donna Morris
Cover and interior design: Jenn Embree

All images are property of Theresa Meuse unless otherwise stated.

Library and Archives Canada Cataloguing in Publication
Meuse, Theresa, 1958-, author
L'nu'k—the people : Mi'kmaw history, culture, and heritage / Theresa Meuse.
    Includes bibliographical references and index.
    ISBN 978-1-77108-452-9 (paperback)
1. Micmac Indians—Atlantic Provinces—Juvenile literature. I. Title.

E99.M6M47 2016   j971.5'00497343   C2016-903748-7

Nimbus Publishing acknowledges the financial support for its publishing activities from the Government of Canada through the Canada Book Fund (CBF) and the Canada Council for the Arts, and from the Province of Nova Scotia. We are pleased to work in partnership with the Province of Nova Scotia to develop and promote our creative industries for the benefit of all Nova Scotians.

This book is dedicated to the Elders who provided me with positive teachings and energy, and who influenced my life's journey. May good spirits continue to guide them all.

The information in this book is based on my Elders' teachings and may differ slightly from another person's teachings.

Msit no'kmaq: all my relations.

Language and Pronunciation

Throughout this book, you will see two spellings of the word **Mi'kmaq**: one ending in a q and one ending in a w. So what's the difference?

MI'KMAQ OR MI'KMAW?

The word **Mi'kmaq** is plural and is also used when referring to the whole nation as a group. For instance: "The **Mi'kmaq** of Eastern Canada."

Mi'kmaw is the singular version of **Mi'kmaq** ("I am **Mi'kmaw**") or an adjective ("A **Mi'kmaw** man told me a story," or "this is a **Mi'kmaw** basket"). **Mi'kmaw** is also used to refer to the language itself. ("She speaks **Mi'kmaw**," or "**Mi'kmaw** is my first language"). So: "All the **Mi'kmaq** spoke **Mi'kmaw** up to the 1950s."

—from *The Language of this Land, Mi'kma'ki* by Trudy Sable and Bernie Francis (2012)

FIRST NATION OR FIRST NATIONS?

I use the term **First Nation** (as opposed to **First Nations**) based on an Elder's explanation that we are all one nation instead of many.

MI'KMA'KI OR ATLANTIC CANADA?

The word **Mi'kma'ki** (mee-ga-mah-gey) is used to describe the territory of the Mi'kmaq. It represents the areas that make up Nova Scotia, Prince Edward Island, Newfoundland, most of New Brunswick, the Gaspé area of Quebec, and the northeastern part of Maine.

PRONUNCIATION

Mi'kmaq is pronounced "meeg-gm-mahh" and **Mi'kmaw** is pronounced "meeg-gm-maaw." The difference is subtle; try reading the words out loud to hear it.

The title of this book, *L'nu'k,* is pronounced "ul-noog," and means "the people." **L'nu** is singular, referring to just one Mi'kmaw person.

Table of Contents

Mi'kmaw artist Brianne Zee's imagining of a traditional community. Note the birchbark wigwams, canoe with raised gunwales, and children helping gather food and cook.

Introduction

Imagine your family and neighbours living in a place like this picture. Your playground and shopping mall is the forest. There are no cars, electric lights, stores, or bicycles. For the most part, you walk everywhere and use a canoe to travel long distances over water. You learn how to take care of your friends and family and the world around you, including the forest and its animals.

Throughout the seasons, families gather to plan hunting and fishing trips. The men and boys set out with the necessary tools—spears, bows and arrows, and sharp tools made from stone—while the women and some Elders stay in the community to watch over the small children, tan animal hides, sew clothing, gather edible plants like berries, and collect firewood. The men might be gone for three or four days, hunting and tracking moose or caribou. You and the other children play in the forest, climbing trees and swimming in the rivers and lakes. You also help pick berries and collect wood for the cooking fires. Everyone living in the community has a job to do, and everyone participates.

This is how the Mi'kmaq, the original settlers of the Maritime provinces, lived long before settlers came to Canada from countries like France and England in the 1500s and 1600s. The Mi'kmaq even had their own government, and each community had a leader known as a *Saqamaw* (sah-ha-mahw), which is the Mi'kmaw word for "respected older person" or "Elder." They had their own language, made their own laws, and knew how to use the plants growing around them to make medicine. They lived in communities that revolved around the idea of sharing with one another.

They called themselves *l'nu'k*, which means "the people." When Europeans started coming to North America, the Mi'kmaq welcomed them with the greeting *nikmaq*, which means "my kin-friends." Settlers from France later borrowed the word and started calling their new First Nation friends *nikmaq*. Over the years, the name became Mi'kmaq.

Descendants of these first peoples still live in the Mi'kmaq traditional territory that is now called Atlantic Canada (New Brunswick, Prince Edward Island, Nova Scotia, Newfoundland, and the Gaspé Peninsula of Quebec). For thousands of years, the Mi'kmaq lived off the land in this region, and called it Mi'kma'ki:

L'nu'k: The People

"Mi'kmaw territory." Most men, women, and children had a deep understanding of the environment— including animals, seasons, weather, landscapes, and waterways—and this understanding is

preserved in their language, history, and stories, which have been passed down from generation to generation, from the beginning of Mi'kmaq time right up to today. But when the Europeans began arriving in the 1500s and 1600s, things changed for the Mi'kmaq.

When Europeans settled in Canada and formed their own government, they called the many tribes of people already living here "Indians," because the explorers thought they had landed in India. And they called the Mi'kmaq "Micmacs," which is the English way to pronounce the word. Today, the Mi'kmaq do not commonly use the names "Indian" and "Micmac," even though the Canadian government still uses "Indian" in its legal documents.

There are many books written about the Mi'kmaq and each one is unique in telling their story. This book will highlight areas of interest to help educate you about Mi'kmaw culture from ancient times to present day. Hopefully, it will encourage you to keep learning more.

CHAPTER 1

Background and Culture

Since the Mi'kmaq lived in Mi'kma'ki long before the first European explorers arrived in the 1500s, they developed a unique and interesting way of life. They knew how to use the land around them to take care of themselves. Read on to find out about their land, homes, food, and traditions as they were before the settlers arrived.

Where The Mi'kmaq Lived

The Mi'kmaq lived in Canada long before the country even got its name. Canada is part of Turtle Island, also known as North America (Canada, the United States, and Mexico). There are many different reasons why North America is called Turtle Island, but the simplest one is that the land is shaped like a turtle. Nova Scotia is located on the front leg of the turtle.

Long ago the Earth was covered in water, and all its creatures lived in the sky or beneath the waves. When it was time for Mother Earth to bring more creatures into the world, she wanted a new place for them to live. The animals wanted to help and told her about the soil far below the water. Once they had the soil, the turtle agreed to support the new land, and Mother Earth placed the soil on its back. As the turtle grew, Mother Earth scattered the seeds of life all over the new land and trees, lakes, flowers, and creatures grew.

Before the Maritime provinces were called Nova Scotia, New Brunswick, and Prince Edward Island, the Mi'kmaq had different names for the areas. Groups of Mi'kmaq lived in areas that are identified with a traditional name in the map on page 8.

L'nu'k: The People

Atlantic Canada As It Was

There were seven main areas throughout Mi'kma'ki, as written in *The Language of this Land, Mi'kma'ki* by Trudy Sable and Bernie Francis:

- *Kespukwitk* pronounced (GES-boo-gweetk): interpreted as "end of flow," which covers the area west of the LaHave River to Yarmouth/Cape Sable in South/Southwestern Nova Scotia.
- *Sipekne'katik/Sikipne'katik* (Su-beh-gn-AYE-gah-dig): interpreted as "area of wild potato or turnip," which covers Shubenacadie and the Minas Basin coast in Nova Scotia.
- *Eskikewa'kik* (Es-gig-eh-WAAH-gig): translation for this word has not been officially determined, but the area covers a portion of the Atlantic coastal region from west of Sheet Harbour to Canso, Nova Scotia.
- *Epekwitk aq Piktuk,* (EH-beh-gwitk ack BIG-toog): interpreted as "cradle above water" and "explosive place," covers Prince Edward Island and the lowland area along the Northumberland Strait, separated from neighbouring districts by the Cobequid Highlands and the Pictou and Antigonish Highlands.

Background and Culture

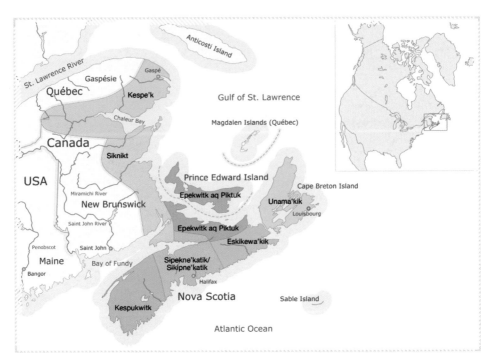

A map of Mi'kma'ki showing how the areas throughout Nova Scotia, New Brunswick, Prince Edward Island, and the Gaspé Peninsula of Quebec were divided up.

- *Unama'kik* (Oon-nah-MAAH-gee): interpreted as a variation of the word Mi'kma'ki, meaning "Mi'kmaw territory," which covers all of Cape Breton Island.
- *Siknikt* (SI-gn-ikt): interpreted as "drainage area," which covers the Miramichi River and Acadian coast and Bay of Fundy region.
- *Kespe'k* (GES-beg): interpreted as "the end" or "land," which covers the Saint John River Valley and the

Appalachian Mountain Range of northern New Brunswick and the Gaspé area of Quebec.

(There is another area the Mi'kmaq call *Ktaqmkuk*, meaning "across the waves/water," which is known today as Newfoundland.)

It is unclear just how many Mi'kmaq lived in Mi'kma'ki during the 1600s and 1700s, but some believe there were many more than today. It is told that Grand Chief Membertou, who lived back in the 1600s, said there were as many Mi'kmaq living as there were hairs on his head. If he was right, that means almost one hundred thousand Mi'kmaq may have lived in the area.

Some people believe the Mi'kmaq ancestors have lived here since the beginning of time, having sprouted from the earth, while others believe they have lived here for over thirteen thousand calendar years. During that time, they would not have been known as "the Mi'kmaq," nor would their way of life been the same as what we read about in the history books today. Plants and animals that are now extinct (like mammoths) would have existed then, meaning a very different lifestyle.

One thing is certain: the Mi'kmaq have lived in Canada for a long, long time.

WIGWAMS

Before the Europeans came across the ocean, the Mi'kmaq travelled all across the land to find, depending on the season, the best hunting and fishing places. The Mi'kmaq made homes in communities that ranged in size. Not all the people lived together in one area; their homes were spaced out along shorelines so every family had access to fresh water. In the winter months, some moved inland into the forests so the trees sheltered them from the winter weather. Starting in spring, they would move back to the ocean shorelines again, following the river closest to their community.

The English word "wigwam" comes from the Mi'kmaw word *wikuom,* which means "she/he/it lives

Todd Labrador, of Acadia First Nation, created this example of a traditional community set-up. Note the birchbark wigwam, canoe, and wooden kettle.

L'nu'k: The People

Modern-day removal of bark from a piece of softwood for making wigwam poles.

there." Wigwams were the traditional Mi'kmaw homes, and were constructed of poles tied together in a cone or A-frame, and then covered in birchbark. It was usually the women who set up the wigwams, and they could put several up in just one day.

The frame of a wigwam was made of tree poles, each 2–10 centimetres thick and as tall at 5 metres. Poles could be collected from trees that had already died (deadwood), trees that had fallen, or smaller softwood trees like cedar, hemlock, or balsam fir. The bark and branches were carefully removed which made the poles smooth and durable. After a couple of years, when the poles became dried out and brittle, they would be replaced.

The size of the wigwam determined how many wooden poles were needed. Poles were cut from trees, tied into a frame with wet spruce root (which tightened up when it dried), and covered on the outside with waterproof

A modern-day birchbark wigwam, as an example of what a traditional Mi'kmaw home would have looked like hundreds of years ago. (*iStock*)

L'nu'k: The People

birchbark. In order to cover the whole structure, the birchbark was layered in pieces starting at the bottom of the wigwam. Each layer was sewn together with spruce root and overlapped so the pieces looked like shingles and kept water out.

Is a Wigwam the Same as a Teepee?

The Mi'kmaq did not use the word "teepee" to describe their homes. That word comes from a different Native language and usually refers to a tent covered in animal skins, not birchbark.

During winter, the Mi'kmaq would build small cooking fires inside their wigwams. Since their diet was so healthy (they ate lots of fresh fish and meat), the natural fats helped keep them warm in colder months and their fires were mainly used to cook food rather than to provide heat. In the summertime, the Mi'kmaq lived outdoors and mainly used the wigwams for shelter on rainy days. Wigwam materials were easy to put together and take apart, so if the Mi'kmaq had to pack up and move they could do it quickly.

Supplies From The Forest

We know our Mi'kmaw ancestors used many things from the forest for different purposes. Lots of these items are still used today, and the following information is based on the Elders' teachings from more modern times.

SPRUCE ROOTS

The stringy roots of spruce trees were commonly used as rope to tie together wigwam poles or help keep the birchbark covering attached to the poles. The roots are very strong and are easy to bend and tie when wet, and tightened up when dry.

Spruce roots could be harvested any time of year when the ground was not frozen. The best place to find good roots that aren't broken or too bent was around swampy bogs. It was easy for the Mi'kmaq to find a clump, pull them up, and coil them into a loop to carry home.

Once enough roots were gathered, each root was split into two equal pieces (if the root was thicker than a man's thumb, the root was split into four pieces). This gave the Mi'kmaq clean, strong material that had many uses: tying wigwam poles together, using as thread for

Todd Labrador (left) holds a bundle of raw spruce root. On the right is what the spruce root looks like after it's been peeled, ready to use as rope or thread.

sewing clothes, shoes, canoes, shingles, or other items. Spruce root is always peeled before using, but if left raw and kept under water, it can be stored for years.

BIRCHBARK

When building wigwams, the Mi'kmaq mainly used bark peeled from birch trees to cover the poles because it was light, waterproof, and lasted a long time. When building temporary shelters, the Mi'kmaq used fir boughs to cover the frame instead of birchbark because they were easier to find and didn't require as much preparation and work.

15

An example of how to remove a small sheet of bark from a birch tree.

L'nu'k: The People

Birchbark for wigwams, tools, or other small items could be cut from the birch tree in all seasons. Some Elders now believe summertime is best because sap helps the bark separate from the trunk, whereas colder temperatures cause the bark to stick to the tree, making it harder to remove in one piece.

Once they selected a tree, the Mi'kmaq used stone knives to cut long, straight lines in the bark. It was important to cut as vertically and straightly as possible, because a horizontal cut all the way around the trunk could kill the tree. To remove the bark, the Mi'kmaq gently worked their hands between it and the trunk, causing the bark to come off in one big sheet, 1–2 metres long.

The outer bark on a birch tree acts as a second skin to the inner bark that protects the tree. If the inner, coarser bark is cut too deep the tree will die, but smaller pieces of birchbark can be removed from the tree without too much damage. Once the outer bark is removed, it never grows back; the inner bark becomes darker and harder instead.

When lots of birchbark was needed—for canoes or large wigwams—the Mi'kmaq simply cut down the whole tree, as the rest of the wood could be used for fires. In order to remove large pieces of bark all at once, several people had to hold the log over a fire to warm the

Todd Labrador (right) and his son show how to remove a big piece of bark from a birch tree to make a Mi'kmaw canoe.

bark and help it separate from the trunk (the way the sap does in summertime).

The bark could be used right away, or stored either rolled up or flattened. When the bark was stored, it would dry out and the Mi'kmaq simply softened it with water when they were ready to use it. Birch trees have a special enzyme that prevents the bark from rotting; another reason it lasts so long and is so valuable.

The Mi'kmaq were (and still are!) very resourceful and knew how to use many things from the forest to help them survive. Besides covering their wigwams, they also used birchbark to make small items like dishes and big things like canoes. The bark is naturally waterproof and very strong.

It wasn't just birchbark, either: the Mi'kmaq knew how to use all sorts of different trees and plants to weave baskets and mix medicines. When they killed an animal for meat, they also used its antlers or bones for buttons and tools, and its fur to make warm clothing. Nothing was wasted and everything served a purpose.

Clothing

Traditional Mi'kmaw clothing was made from animal hides and furs, which were layered as the seasons got colder. After an animal was killed and its meat and bones removed, the Mi'kmaq would clean, stretch, and smoke (drying it over the smoke from a fire) the skin to make soft leather. They would use pointy, sharpened bones (awls) to make holes in the leather for sewing and adding decoration. Animal sinew, the stringy tissue between muscles and bones, was separated into strands and used as thread.

Each group of First Nation people has their own way to decorate their belongings. The unique Mi'kmaw

19

A traditional Mi'kmaw woman's cap, showing the double-curve motif. *(Nova Scotia Archives)*

design looks like a line with two curly ends. This design is painted or sewn on clothing, canoes, and wigwams. No one knows for sure what this design represents, but the Mi'kmaq have used it for as long as anyone can remember. Alan Syliboy, a modern Mi'kmaw artist, describes the double curve as being "the symbol for life. A fern starts as a tight fist and opens as life begins and continues to grow." Bernie Francis, a Mi'kmaw linguist, points out that, just like the Inukshuk is symbolic to the Inuit, the double-curved design is symbolic to the Mi'kmaq. This design is even recognizable in the ancient petroglyph drawings on page 35. Porcupine quills are another popular choice for decoration since they are strong and can be bent into the curved design.

Before the Europeans arrived, the Mi'kmaq decorated their clothes with shells, feathers, beads made out of antler and bone, and other things that nature provided. They could even make their own dyes using plants

L'nu'k: The People

A portrait from around 1865 showing traditional Mi'kmaw dress. Note the curly motif on the woman's cap. (*Nova Scotia Archives*)

(roots, bark, leaves, or flowers). The best paintbrush was a moose's shin bone, since it was naturally very fatty and didn't allow the paint to get chunky.

When the Europeans arrived, the Mi'kmaq began trading their furs and meat for European cloth, ribbon, and glass beads. With these new materials, they found ways to accent their traditional designs. Over time, the Mi'kmaq started using imported cotton, linen, and wool for their clothing instead of skins, but they always kept their signature curly pattern. Today, the Mi'kmaq use mainly manufactured leather for ceremonial clothing, but beads, shells, and feathers are still used for decorating clothing and footwear.

MKSNK—MOCCASINS

Handmade leather moccasins, decorated with leather strips and beads.

Shoes and boots, which the Mi'kmaq called *mksnk* (mee-geese-sink; "moccasins" in English), were made from two pieces of either caribou or moose hide. One piece formed the bottom shoe-piece, and the vamp, or tongue, covered the top of the foot. Moccasins were worn all year round and stretched to fit the person's foot the more they wore them. Though they were worn in all types of weather, shoes were designed depending on the season.

In the summertime, moccasins were a shoe shape, fitting to the ankle. In the winter months, moccasins were

Did You Know?

The large feathered headdresses worn by some First Nation people are not part of traditional Mi'kmaw clothing. Large headdresses, like those worn by the nations in the prairie lands of central-west Canada (such as the Cree Nation) would have been difficult to wear in the forests of Mi'kma'ki; the feathers likely would have gotten caught in all the branches. Mi'kmaw men wear a simple headband that might have had one feather or several sewn onto it. This headwear is worn during times of celebration and gatherings.

more boot-like; they fit closer to the knees and were lined with removable strips of rabbit fur, making them warmer. When they weren't being worn, children would take out the fur strips and hang them to dry so the lining wouldn't get stinky and wet. Moccasins were waterproof and very strong, and each pair could last for a couple of years.

Food

Before European settlers arrived, Mi'kma'ki looked very different than it does today: the land was covered in forests that were full of moose, caribou, and porcupines. The rivers and lakes were bursting with fish, and along the shores of the ocean lived huge herds of seals and walrus. The skies were crowded with birds.

Since the Mi'kmaq spent most of the year along the coast, they ate many types of fish, birds, and eggs. They could catch a lot of different seafood: eels, salmon, and trout in the spring; cod, oysters, and lobster in the summer; smelt, more eels, and herring in the fall; walrus or seal on the winter ice.

Fish was not the only staple in the Mi'kmaw diet: meat like caribou, beaver, partridge, and porcupine was also abundant and full of nutrients. Usually, the meat was

23

cooked over an open fire. If there was a lot of meat that needed to be preserved, the Mi'kmaq often used smoke from a cooking fire to create a coating on the meat and fish, making it last longer. Today, many people still smoke fish and meat in buildings called smokehouses.

The Mi'kmaq also picked berries and plants from spring to fall. All the berries—like wild blueberries, cranberries, or strawberries—had lots of vitamins and helped keep everyone healthy. Some specific roots were used for flour, as ingredients in soups, and sometimes eaten raw (groundnut). Plants like sweet flag, goldenthread, and alder could be picked and used to

Eel Weirs

Eel weirs consisted of wooden stakes or large rocks stuck in the muddy riverbed with branches woven between them to form a wall. This blocked the way out, and forced the eels to swim into the trap.

Eels travel once a year from freshwater streams and lakes to the saltwater ocean to lay their eggs (this is called "spawning"), before heading back the way they came. This gave the Mi'kmaq two chances to catch them: once on the way upriver to the ocean in spring, and again in the fall on the way back downriver. Today, spawning cycles have slowed down because of things like human-made dams, pollution, and too much fishing.

A hollowed-out log (*apitakwijit*) used as a wooden kettle for cooking.

make medicine. (You can read more about the traditional plants in Chapter Three.)

Open fires were not just for cooking meat: the Mi'kmaq also used the flames to bake bread, which the Mi'kmaq now call *luski* (loo-ski), which is short for *lu'sknikn*. All the ingredients came from the forest and could have included acorns or roots from plants ground up to make a powder just like flour. Elders taught younger Mi'kmaq how to make luski by showing them and not by using a written recipe. Today, luski-making is still taught the same way.

Another method of cooking was to use a hollowed-out tree log as a wooden kettle. This is known by some

How To Make Luski

Over the years, the ingredients for making luski have changed and today we use modern elements. Although there is no exact recipe, here is an example of how you can try to make luski:

- Preheat the oven to 350°F.
- In a big bowl, mix together 6 cups flour and 3 heaping tablespoons of baking powder.
- Make a bowl shape with one hand and add enough salt in the centre of your palm to fill the small hole. Some people add 2 teaspoons of sugar but it is not necessary. Add salt (and sugar if you're using it) to the flour mixture and stir.
- Make a hole in the center of your dry mixture to the bottom of the bowl so it looks like a volcano. Add enough cold water to fill the hole and have the water spread out over the top of the flour mixture until almost covered. Mix with a spoon until moistened and a bit sticky.
- Sprinkle some flour on a clean, dry cutting board or countertop. Take the dough out of the bowl and place on floured surface. Push the dough back and forth with your hands (knead) until it is not too crumbly and dry or sticky.
- You can divide your dough ball into loaves or leave it as one big loaf. Grease a cookie sheet with a bit of butter or oil and place the ball on top, flattening it a bit to make it nearly the same size from end to end. Take a knife and cut lines on the top of each loaf but not too deep in the dough.
- Bake in the oven at 350° for about an hour until golden brown on top. Sometimes it takes longer depending on the size. Ripping the loaf in two will allow you to see if it is cooked all the way through. If it's not quite finished and still a bit sticky in the middle, just place back into the oven until it's fully baked. When it is done, lightly rub butter on the sides, top, and bottom.
- Now you're ready to enjoy! Luski tastes great with molasses.

L'nu'k: The People

Mi'kmaq as a *apitakwijit* (aba-dah-gwee-jeet), which means "to turn over." Since the log was too heavy to carry around, it was turned over when not in use and left in seasonal camps to use at a later time.

To make a wooden kettle, a piece of a tree trunk was hollowed out using fire and stone tools, and then filled with water. Then, stones were heated in a fire and placed in the log's water to help it boil. Food was placed directly in the water, allowing it to cook. Since the log would catch fire if placed directly on the flames, it was usually kept just to the side of the fire so the heated rocks could be easily transferred from the fire to the kettle.

Transportation

CANOES

Different First Nation cultures on Turtle Island have their own way to build canoes. The shape of a traditional Mi'kmaw canoe is unique because the front (bow) and back (stern) curve upward instead of lying flat against the water. There are two types of Mi'kmaw canoes: an ocean-going canoe and a river-going canoe. The middle of an ocean-going canoe has one raised section in the middle called a gunwale. This stops the waves from splashing

Ocean

gunwale

River

bow

stern

➤GERALD-GLOADE➤

Illustrations showing the different shapes of Mi'kmaw canoes. (*Gerald Gloade*)

up over the sides. Canoes made for travelling over flat water (like rivers, lakes, or streams) do not have raised gunwales, but do have the curved bow and stern. These features make Mi'kmaw canoes very fast in the water.

Canoes were usually between 3 and 8 metres long and featured a wooden frame wrapped in waterproof birchbark, just like the wigwams. These design features made the Mi'kmaw canoe extremely light and easy to carry, but also swift and

Did You Know?

Mi'kmaw canoe-builders always place the birchbark so the white side of the bark faces the inside of the canoe and the smooth, beige side of the bark (the most water resistant) faces out. Since the white bark is so pretty, some movies, television shows, or artists show canoes and wigwams "inside-out" because they aren't aware of this design fact.

L'nu'k: The People

A modern-day birchbark canoe built by Todd Labrador.

safe for the water. The canoes could hold several hundred pounds (two or three grown-ups) and were so well built, they could travel on rivers, lakes, or even the Atlantic Ocean.

Canoes started out as several big pieces of birchbark, which were then sewn together with wet spruce root. In order to keep water from leaking into the canoe where the stitches were, the Mi'kmaq made their own waterproof filler: a mixture of sticky balsam-fir gum, animal fat, and charcoal. These ingredients were mixed together, melted over a fire, and then applied to the seams in the birchbark. The sticky mixture hardened and dried very quickly, so canoe-builders had to know exactly what they were doing and work briskly to not waste anything.

Building canoes and mixing homemade, waterproof filler are both good examples of how the Mi'kmaq were scientists and chemists such a long time ago. They knew the exact measurements required to make a canoe float and how to mix different natural substances to make it reliable and waterproof. Not every Mi'kmaq could make a good birchbark canoe; it was hard work and required patience and knowledge. It became a specialized craft that some people learned and passed on to others. They became known as canoe builders.

Although a few people throughout Mi'kma'ki make birchbark canoes today, one of the most well known is Todd Labrador of the Acadia First Nation in Nova Scotia. He continues to make and teach about traditional canoes on a regular basis, using the same science and chemistry as his ancestors.

SNOWSHOES

Even today, travel can be difficult when there is a lot of ice and snow. When the Mi'kmaq went hunting in wintertime hundreds of years ago, they needed special shoes to help them stay on top of the snow rather than sinking down into it. These snowshoes were perfect for walking long distances because it didn't take as much energy to walk through big snow drifts.

Snowshoes look a bit like tennis rackets: oval-shaped in front with a handle in back. The frame is wooden, usually yellow birch or maple, with two crosspieces to hold the

Snowshoes look like tennis rackets, but make it possible to walk on top of snow.

snowshoe-wearer's weight. Across the frame, the Mi'kmaq stretched strips of rawhide (made from the hide of a moose or caribou, but not tanned like leather) to create meshing. Rawhide was better than leather for snowshoes as it wouldn't get soggy and stretched out when wet.

The same calculations used hundreds of years ago are still used today: the size of the snowshoe mesh depends on weather conditions. For example: tighter, smaller mesh is good for walking through loose, powdery snow; the snow simply falls through the holes. Wider mesh is better for wet snow because the snow gets clumpy and sticks on top of the shoes; the wider holes allow the clumps of snow to fall through.

Making snowshoes for each individual was another example of how the Mi'kmaq used math: they had to know a person's height, weight, and shoe size, as well as the type of snow the person needed to traverse, in order to calculate the size of the meshing so the wearer could stay on top of the snow.

Background and Culture

SLEDS

Since the Mi'kmaq travelled on foot most of the time, carrying heavy loads was difficult. They crafted wooden *tepagns* (tab-a-kins), similar to an Inuit dogsled, for hauling their belongings across snow and ice. The wide, flat runners were usually made of a hard wood like rock maple, and slid easily across the frozen ground. A person could pull more than 400 pounds on a sled, and women sometimes used them to haul home pieces of the moose or caribou the men hunted and killed.

Language and Communication

WAMPUM BELT

Today, we can communicate with each other by using a telephone or computer. Hundreds of years ago, the Mi'kmaq had their own method of communication. They used a leather belt with coloured shells sewn on it, relaying stories of the treaties or other messages. This belt, called a wampum belt, was passed back and forth within Mi'kma'ki, like a letter.

Some used purple shells that came from quahog clams, and white ones that came from whelks (sea

Wampum belts of different sizes to relay messages. *(University of Toronto)*

snails). One person was assigned to be the runner or belt keeper, and he or she was responsible for looking after the belt and for taking it to neighbouring communities so they could learn the story or message. Sometimes, the belt might have told the history of the Mi'kmaw people, sent a marriage proposal, or been offered as a gift. Some very old wampum belts are displayed in Mi'kmaw cultural centres or museums.

PETROGLYPHS

Petroglyphs are drawings or etchings in stone that can tell us things about the life of the Mi'kmaq. For example, some petroglyphs show animals, stars, a person fishing, plants, and even drawings of European ships that came to this area long ago. They acted like a modern newspaper: giving information about what was happening in everyday life, telling stories of people who lived long ago, and serving as memory aids.

Petroglyphs Versus Hieroglyphs

Petroglyphs are very old images—drawings of people, animals, or events—carved into rocks. Hieroglyphs are very similar: pictures that represent words, sounds, or ideas and are drawn on birchbark, fabric, or wood instead of rock. Both can be found throughout Canada and other parts of the world.

In Nova Scotia, Kejimkujik National Park and National Historic Site and the Bedford Barrens both have rocks still showing these old drawings. There are over five hundred individual etchings in Kejimkujik National Park alone. These areas are protected sites and people can visit them, but only at certain times of the year. The petroglyphs have become protected areas because people had been drawing over them, not knowing how important they are to history. Rain and snow also slowly wash away the petroglyphs, causing river ice to scrape along the stone. To make sure the drawings will never be lost, historians have made sure to take pictures to preserve the drawings for future generations.

L'nu'k: The People

Petroglyphs showing different aspects of Mi'kmaw life. There are more than 500 of these drawings in Kejimkujik alone! (*Images courtesy of Donna Morris, taken at Kejimkujik National Park and Historic Site, Nova Scotia*)

MI'KMAW LANGUAGE

Before the arrival of the Europeans, the Mi'kmaw language wasn't written in words or sentences. These days, we use the English alphabet to help create the sounds in their language. Today's Mi'kmaw alphabet is made up of eleven consonants: j, k, l, m, n, p, q, s, t, w, and y. There are also eleven vowels: a, e, i, o, u and a', e', i', o', u', and a vowel known as a *schwa*, which looks like an i with a line through it: ɨ.

The language itself is very descriptive. For example, the word for the month of May is *Tquoljewiku's*, which means "frog-croaking moon," and the word for February is *Apiknajit*, which means "snow-blinding month." The words often describe sights, sounds, and smells—the experience or feeling—rather than being named after something or someone.

Here are some basic Mi'kmaw words and popular names, along with a guide of how to pronounce them. As with any language, there are always slight variations in spelling and pronunciation. The following words use the Smith-Francis Orthography (the most commonly accepted spelling of the Mi'kmaw language) to spell Mi'kmaw words with the English alphabet.

L'nu'k: The People

Thank you (to one person) . . . *wela'lin* (weh-lah-lyn)

Thank you (to a group) . . . . *wela'lioq* (weh-lah-lee-oh)

You're welcome . . . . . . *weliaq* (weh-lee-yah)

Hello . . . . *kwe'* (kway-or-gway)

See you later. . . . . *nmu'ltes* (na-mole-dis)

Welcome . . . . *pjila'si* (up-jee-lah-see)

NAMES

Matthew . . . . *Mattio* (mad-ee-oo)

Michael . . . . *Mise'l* (mee-sell)

Thomas . . . . *Tuma* (doo-mah)

William . . . . *Sulia'n* (soo-lee-un)

Theresa . . . . *San'tele's* (san-dah-lez)

Mary . . . . *Mali* (mah-lee)

Rose . . . . *Lo's* (lows)

Helen . . . . *Elen* (ay-lan)

ANIMALS

Bear . . . . *muin* (moo-in)

Deer . . . . *lentuk* (len-took or len-doog)

Porcupine . . . . *matues* (mah-doo-ehs)

Eagle . . . . *kitpu* (geedt-poo, or boo)

SEASONS

Spring . . . . *sikw* (see-uk)

Summer . . . . *nipk* (neepk)

Fall . . . . *toqewa'q* (doh-wah)

Winter . . . . *kesik* (gehs-ick)

NUMBERS

One . . . . *ne'wt* (nay-out)

Two . . . . *ta'pu* (dah-boo)

Three . . . . *si'st* (seest)

Four . . . . *ne'w* (nay-oh)

Five . . . . *na'n* (nahn)

FOODS

Milk . . . . *mlakej* (mulh-ah-gehde)

Bread . . . . *piqnaqn* (bib-nah-hun)

Water . . . . *samqwan* (sum-hwon)

Salt . . . . *salawey* (sah-lah-way)

Pepper . . . . *te'pi'sewey* (deh-bees-a-way)

Potato . . . . *tapatat* (dah-bah-dah)

Entertainment and Leisure

WALTES

A modern handcrafted waltes board, game pieces, and scoring sticks.

The Mi'kmaq had many ways to relax and have some fun. A popular game called waltes was one everyone enjoyed. To play, two to six people (maybe more) sat in a circle around a wooden plate. Little round bone pieces with markings on one side were placed in the plate. Each person took a turn gently tapping the plate on the ground, trying to make the bone pieces flip. The more pieces turned up the same way, the more points you scored. Players received long, slender sticks to represent points earned.

Waltes is still played the same way today, although buying the game dish, bone pieces, and scoring sticks can be expensive. This is mainly due to the type of wood (sometimes rock maple) and special skill needed to make the game.

STORYTELLING

Storytelling was another favourite pastime of the Mi'kmaq. It was both entertaining and helped hand down knowledge through generations. Everyone enjoyed sharing stories with one another, and many became known as storytellers. A good storyteller was able to speak to any age group and teach a lesson. A storyteller would know lots of teachings about different things: people, relationships, animals, spirits, Mother Earth, weather, and nature. While many stories made people laugh, there was always a lesson to be learned about life. Mi'kmaw storytelling is still popular today. See page 79 for an example of a traditional Mi'kmaw story.

Crafts and Artifacts

During the 1600s and 1700s, the Mi'kmaq were known for their skill and talent for making many things by hand. Since they didn't have shopping malls or corner stores to purchase pre-made goods, they had to learn to make everything they wanted or needed from the materials around them. These craft-making skills are still taught today. What follows are a few of the more common items, some of which became more popular after the Europeans arrived and began trading with the Mi'kmaq.

WOVEN BASKETS

Traditionally, Mi'kmaw baskets were made to carry and store food and other items. When they moved for the season, collected materials from the forest, or gathered food, the Mi'kmaq wore their baskets like a backpack. It was important that the baskets were sturdy and of good quality so they wouldn't fall apart and scatter the things they held.

Centuries ago, various types of trees and roots would have been used to make baskets. Today, they are most commonly made from the wood of ash trees. The first step to making a basket was to visit the forest to find the perfect tree: it needed to be free of knots, twists, or any marks that might affect the growth-ring pattern on the inside. It was (and still is) Mi'kmaw tradition to not take anything from the environment without giving thanks to Kisu'lkw (gis-ool-kew), the Creator, and thanking the spirit of the tree for giving up its life. It is also a good way to give back to what Mother Earth provides. Today, some Mi'kmaq might leave ceremonial tobacco or another sacred medicine on the ground as an offering wherever a

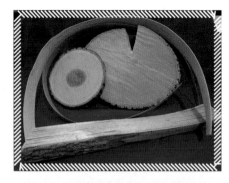

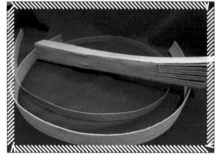

The stages of pounding out the ash wood to make splints for weaving.

tree is cut down.

Today's baskets are still made the same traditional way. Once the tree is cut down, its pieces are split in halves, quarters, or maybe eighths depending on the width of the ribbon-like pieces needed for the basket. One of the reasons ash trees are the best for making baskets is because when it is lightly pounded, ash wood separates at each growth ring; these pieces are called splints. A special knife is used to remove brittle pieces from the splint, making the wood smoother and easier to weave. It takes days to make a true Mi'kmaw basket, and involves going to the forest to find the right tree, cutting it down, bringing it home, pounding out the splints, organizing the tools and materials, weaving the splints, adding a handle or cover, and preparing the extra touches (like dying the splints different colors or collecting and weaving sweetgrass into the basket).

A collection of woven ash baskets. On the far left is a backpack, and on the right is a fishing creel. Those in the middle are hand-held baskets.

Some popular names of baskets are fishing creels, backpacks, fancy baskets, and berry, potato, or apple baskets. Both men and women can make baskets and each one is unique to his or her style and decoration.

When the Europeans arrived in Turtle Island, they found the baskets very beautiful and useful. Even today, Mi'kmaw ash baskets are popular. Each one is unique in its design and size, and can be easily repaired if it gets a hole or starts to split. Some Mi'kmaw baskets stored in museums have been reported to last for hundreds of years.

QUILLWORK

A sample of using porcupine quills to decorate small birchbark containers.
(*Nova Scotia Archives*)

Since the Mi'kmaq had no storage closets or kitchen cabinets to keep their things in, baskets and other types of containers were important to help stay organized and transport their belongings. One of the most popular containers was made of birchbark sewn together with spruce roots. If it were stitched tightly enough, a birchbark box would even hold water. To make it unique, birchbark could be decorated with coloured porcupine quills to make designs and patterns.

Porcupine quillwork was something the Mi'kmaq were especially good at. Porcupine quills are naturally white with black tips, but they were easy to dye. With a bit of water, the quills were also easy to bend and fit into pre-made holes in the birchbark container (or leather if they were decorating clothing).

Because the porcupine quills were very small and narrow, the crafter had to have a good eye for detail, steady hands, and lots of patience. Often, a quill might snap or not quite fit in the hole. Each intricate design was original, but one thing was the same for each container: hours of hard work.

Today, porcupine quills can be collected without hurting the animal. Simply place a wool blanket over the porcupine and then lift it off; some quills will stick to the blanket, and the animal will not be harmed.

WOODEN FLOWERS

No one is quite sure how long the Mi'kmaq have been making decorative wooden flowers, they seem to be more of a modern use of the forest. Made from the wood of a poplar or aspen tree, each piece is shaved

A collection of handcrafted wooden flowers made from poplar wood.

Background and Culture

down to a paper-like thinness before being shaped into a flower. The wood is then coloured with natural or store-bought dyes.

Some enjoy making modern blossoms such as roses, tulips, and carnations, while others prefer wildflowers like buttercups, apple blossoms, or black-eyed Susans. Some create traditional flowers like starflower and lady's slipper. Used for decorative purposes, each wooden flower is unique and lasts a very long time.

JEWELLERY

Traditionally, Mi'kmaw jewellery consisted mainly of necklaces and bracelets made from leather, shells, porcupine quills, animal bones, antlers, or claws. These would have mainly been worn during special gatherings and ceremonies, and some were likely given as gifts.

Once European settlers arrived, they brought modern materials like glass beads and wire, and these became part of Mi'kmaw crafting. Some traditional materials are still used today: dyed porcupine quills for earrings and necklaces; bones, beads, and shells for special clothing like regalia. Today's jewellery helps showcase the combination of modern materials and traditional skills.

Things like bear-claw necklaces or medicine pouches are not necessarily viewed as pieces of jewellery and are better known as sacred medicines—something to make you feel happy and safe (see page 73). They are usually considered a spiritual connector and are not always displayed for others to see. It is a sign of disrespect to wear these things for showing-off purposes.

CANOE PADDLES AND AXE HANDLES

After European settlers arrived, they relied on the paddles and other wooden tools the Mi'kmaq made. Paddles were made in different sizes and weights

The view from the inside of a birchbark canoe on the water, along with a handcrafted canoe paddle.

Background and Culture

An Elder's Axe-handle Story

Since the ash tree was becoming scarce and its wood was heavy and hard, carving axe handles took a very long time. The Mi'kmaq had to begin charging more for them because of this. Buyers didn't like having to pay the higher price, so the Mi'kmaq made less expensive handles using wood from poplar trees. Poplar was more plentiful but not as strong as ash. Unfortunately, the poplar handles did not last as long. This meant the buyers had to return more often to buy more handles from the Elders, which made the Elders happy.

depending on the height of the person and the body of water they planned to use it in. For example, if the person liked to stand when paddling, the paddle would have to be longer and may have a wider blade. If the person would be paddling in calmer waters like a small lake, the paddle may be more lightweight and narrow.

Men's paddles were typically made from heavy rock maple, which is better for steering the canoe in rough water. Women and non-Mi'kmaw paddlers used lighter wood, like ash. Sometimes paddles were decorated with carved or painted designs, but most were left natural. To view Mi'kmaw paddles in person, visit the Maritime Museum of the Atlantic in Halifax or the visitors' centre at Kejimkujik National Park.

Along with canoe paddles, the Mi'kmaq were also skilled at crafting beautiful, durable axe handles, a skill many still practice today. Axe handles would have become most popular just after European settlers began arriving with axe bits and other tools (like saws and hammers) that required handles. Using ash, the Mi'kmaq carved handles to fit any size axe or tool. Along with woven baskets, the Mi'kmaq made lots of paddles and handles to sell or trade.

CHAPTER 2

Modern Mi'kmaw History

ife for the Mi'kmaq before European arrival was based on cultural teachings and lifestyles passed down through generations. When the Europeans began arriving in Mi'kma'ki in the 1600s they brought their own culture, which was foreign to the Mi'kmaq and (in most cases) had a negative effect on them.

A watercolour painting showing a Mi'kmaw camp at Point Levi in Quebec from around 1838–1842. (*Library & Archives Canada*)

European materials like glass beads, silk, cotton, and metal pots and pans were positive and useful, the settlers' way of life impacted the Mi'kmaq in less positive ways. For example, diseases like smallpox and tuberculosis came off the boats with the settlers and since the Mi'kmaq never had to deal with these illnesses, they had no knowledge of cures, and their bodies could not cope. A very big portion of the Mi'kmaw population (90 percent!) died.

As more French and English settlers arrived and claimed property, the Mi'kmaq had less access to forests, beaches, rivers, and lakes. Less hunting, fishing, and gathering of traditional medicines meant less food and clothing and other things the Mi'kmaq needed to survive. More died from poverty and starvation.

The Mi'kmaq did not separate land into privately owned plots; to them, no one "owned" the land. When these European settlers told the Mi'kmaq they could no longer hunt or fish in the waters and lands, it caused confusion. The new British government did not want First Nation people interfering with its plans to develop Canada, so it created laws to control First Nation people across the country. A law called the Indian Act established things like reserves and Residential Schools.

Canadian Laws for the First Nation

THE INDIAN ACT

Imagine the government telling your family and everyone in your community where and how to live, where you could go to school or travel. Imagine they decided the way you were living was "wrong" and it needed to change. This is what happened when the Canadian government made a law called the Indian Act in 1876.

The act was a set of rules the government created and presented as "law," and it was forced onto First Nation people throughout Canada. The government thought it would benefit them, but actually it ended up doing the opposite. It meant First Nation people could no longer make their own decisions about their government, live the way they were used to living, speak their own language, or practice their cultural teachings (like the smudging, drumming, or sweat lodge ceremonies discussed in the next chapter). Even though the Indian Act has been around since 1876, the government did not even consider First Nation people to be Canadian citizens until 1956.

The Indian Act is still in use today, and no other group of people in Canada is governed by such a law.

RESERVES

As far back as the early 1600s, European settlers began taking over more and more land throughout Mi'kma'ki. One of the first places the French settled and developed was Port Royal in western Nova Scotia. French explorer Samuel de Champlain and his men started building a fort there in 1605.

Port Royal was an area where the Mi'kmaq already lived, as it was close to the ocean but sheltered: it provided everything they needed. When the French settlers moved in, the Mi'kmaq no longer had sole use of the land and water, but they did not mind sharing. This helped build a good relationship between the Mi'kmaq and the French. As a result of that friendship, French missionaries baptized the Mi'kmaw leader Chief Membertou and several of his family members into the Catholic faith. Many of the Mi'kmaq followed suit. Today, Catholicism is still the most common religion among the Mi'kmaq.

Being kind and generous, the Mi'kmaq continued to welcome new settlers to Mi'kma'ki as they arrived. The Mi'kmaq understood that no one owned the land; anyone was allowed to live on it as long as he or she took only what was needed.

Modern Mi'kmaw History

It was during the 1700s, as more and more Europeans came to live on the beautiful coastal lands in Mi'kma'ki, that the Mi'kmaq and their traditional ways of life were being squeezed onto smaller plots of land. The English and French were fighting in Europe, and when they came to Turtle Island they continued to fight for control of the country that was being built here. Unfortunately, the Mi'kmaw were caught in the middle. Settlers from England believed they knew what was best for the Mi'kmaq and encouraged them to follow the Catholic religion, adopt a European lifestyle, and speak English.

By the early 1800s, the British government had taken control of most of the lands and waterways of Mi'kma'ki and decided to set aside plots of land just for First Nation people. They called these areas "reserves." On these lands, many families were forced to live in one area rather than spread out like they were used to. Some land bases were as small as one hundred acres and others as large as one thousand acres. The land the government set aside for the reserves was not always the best; many were located in swampy areas, on rocky hills, or had soil that was like clay. Since the Mi'kmaq were placed on these lands, it was harder for them to fish, hunt, or harvest medicines. The government didn't seem to care

L'nu'k: The People

about the health of the Mi'kmaq and wanted only to control them by gathering them in one spot, like farmers herd their cattle. This set-up did not help the Mi'kmaq or other First Nation people lead healthy lifestyles.

Today, nearly half of all First Nation people in Canada live on reserve lands. As a result of the historical hardship placed on the Mi'kmaq by the European government, the present-day federal government continues to work with First Nation people to help improve their lifestyles. Depending on where they're located, some reserves have been able to create job opportunities for their residents. The communities established on reserves that are closer to main highways, for example, may have more stores, garages, movie theatres, and hotels, because their location allows for more general public, like tourists and passers-by. Other reserves are more isolated from the general public, and this prevents businesses from being developed. Rural reserves have to rely on their community members and local people to keep their businesses going.

RESIDENTIAL SCHOOLS

Imagine a strange man, known as an Indian Agent, and a police officer coming to your home and telling your parents the government has decided you will attend a school that is far away from your home and family. There, you will learn a different culture and speak a different language. These men call it a "residential school" and they take you with them right away—you have no time to get your clothes, favourite toys, snacks, or even a blanket. This happened in First Nation communities all over Canada for more than one hundred years. In all, about 150,000 children were removed from their homes between the 1830s and the 1990s.

Your parents don't have a choice in the matter. Maybe it makes them feel better when the Indian Agent tells them

wonderful opportunities are available for you at the residential school. Even if your parents don't want you to go, it makes no difference: the government has already made the decision for them.

A picture of the Shubenacadie Residential School in Nova Scotia, which has since been torn down. (*Isabelle Knockwood*)

L'nu'k: The People

This tree is in the field where the Shubenacadie Residential School used to stand.
(*Chris Benjamin*)

The school has bedrooms as well as classrooms and a kitchen, so you live there for the whole school year. Depending on your age, you could be there for one to five years; most children stayed until they turned sixteen. If you have brothers and sisters, you might be brought to the school together, but once you arrive, you're separated. You are punished if you speak the language you spoke at home. Your hair is cut short, you wear only the clothes given to you by the adults running the school, eat food you're not familiar with, and attend lessons taught in a language you don't understand. You hardly ever get to see your parents and family. On top of your studies, you have to do many

Day Schools

In the late 1800s and early 1900s, the Canadian government built many small, one-room schoolhouses on reserves for Mi'kmaw children. The teachers at these schools did not teach the Mi'kmaw culture, or even speak the Mi'kmaw language. The European style of education was foreign to the Mi'kmaw students, so attendance was not always high. The government eventually closed the day schools.

Today, there are many First Nation communities with on-reserve schools ranging from primary to grade twelve. These schools are owned and operated by the Mi'kmaq and include First Nation cultural teachings as well as the subjects learned in other schools like math, science, and physical education.

chores and hard, physical labour. If you do not obey the teachers and their strict rules, you are punished.

The purpose of the schools was to force the students to lose their First Nation cultural teachings and learn only European ways. In Atlantic Canada, Mi'kmaw children attended the residential school located in Shubenacadie, Nova Scotia. By the time they left the school, most of the students were teenagers. They no longer spoke the Mi'kmaw language, they did not feel close to their family members, they forgot what it was like to live in a community, and they no longer understood (or were afraid to practice) traditional Mi'kmaw teachings.

L'nu'k: The People

The view across the Shubenacadie River, to the site where the school used to be. It is now home to a plastic factory. (*Chris Benjamin*)

Imagine what it would be like to return back to your family and community after spending a year at a school like that. Would things be the same or different? Some children even felt like strangers in their own communities. Because it was so painful, no one talked about the school.

Although the Shubenacadie Residential School closed in 1967, it has only been in the last few decades that some students, who are now adults, have started to share their stories. In 2008, Prime Minister Stephen Harper made a public apology on behalf of the Canadian government to the First Nation people who attended the residential and day schools across the country.

The government also created a program to help First Nation people heal from the punishments received while attending the schools, and to make up for the loss of their culture. There is still a lot pain, but by sharing their stories, the healing for residential school survivors has finally begun.

CENTRALIZATION

For many years the Mi'kmaq lived on various reserves spread throughout Mi'kma'ki, and the Maliseet people, a First Nation with its own customs and culture, lived in northern New Brunswick. In 1942, the federal government decided all Mi'kmaw and Maliseet people should live on one of four reserves: two in Nova Scotia (Shubenacadie and Eskasoni), and two in New Brunswick (Tobique and Big Cove). The government thought having all the Mi'kmaq and Maliseet people centralized in fewer areas would make it easier to control them. The Mi'kmaq and Maliseet were promised new homes and good jobs if they agreed to move.

Many families did end up moving and this is one of the main reasons why these selected reserves have the largest populations in Mi'kma'ki. The families that did

1420307		

CERTIFICATE OF INDIAN STATUS · CERTIFICAT DE STATUT D'INDIEN

	Date of birth - Date de naissance	Registry group - Groupe d'enregistrement
Your Picture Here	Dec.15,1970 PEIGAN	
DOE	Sex - Sexe M	This card is valid until Cette carte est valide jusqu'au ▶ Apr.26,2002
JOHN CARL	Holder's signature - Signature du titulaire	
JOHNNY	*John C. Doe*	
4360000000	Issuing officer's signature - Signature de l'agent émetteur	Issue date - Date d'émission Apr.26,1997

Even though there have been several cards created over the last few years, this older-style of "Certificate of Indian Status" card given to First Nation people by the Government of Canada seems to be the most widely used in Mi'kma'ki.

move soon learned there were no nice homes or jobs waiting for them. When word got back to others, many families refused to leave their communities. In 1950, the government gave up this plan and the number of reserves remained, with a few more added since then.

You can review the map on the next page to see how many reserves there currently are in the Atlantic provinces.

BILL C-31

The Indian Act is a law that decides whom is considered a "First Nation" person living in Canada. Each First Nation person is then given an identification card known as a Certificate of Indian Status.

Before 1985, the Canadian government had a rule that discriminated against First Nation women: if, for example,

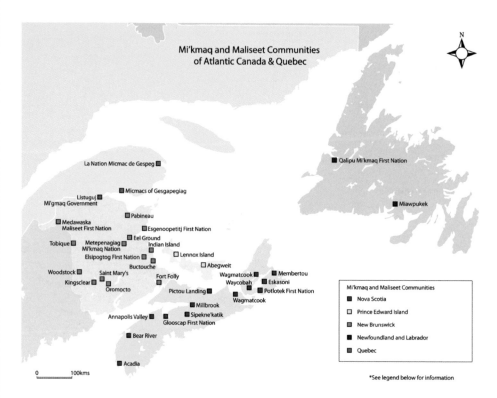

Mi'kmaq and Maliseet Communities
of Atlantic Canada & Quebec

La Nation Micmac de Gespeg

Qalipu Mi'kmaq First Nation

Micmacs of Gesgapegiag

Listuguj
Mi'gmaq Government

Miawpukek

Pabineau

Medawaska
Maliseet First Nation

Esgenoopetitj First Nation

Eel Ground

Tobique   Metepenagiag   Indian Island
Mi'kmaq Nation

Elsipogtog First Nation   Lennox Island

Buctouche   Abegweit

Woodstock   Saint Mary's   Wagmatcook   Membertou

Kingsclear   Fort Folly   Waycobah   Eskasoni

Oromocto   Pictou Landing   Potlotek First Nation

Wagmatcook

Millbrook

Annapolis Valley   Sipekne'katik
Glooscap First Nation

Bear River

Acadia

Mi'kmaq and Maliseet Communities
■ Nova Scotia
☐ Prince Edward Island
■ New Brunswick
■ Newfoundland and Labrador
■ Quebec

0   100kms

*See legend below for information

This map shows all the Mi'kmaq and Maliseet communities throughout Mi'kma'ki. Check the legend on the next page to see each band and its reserves throughout Mi'kma'ki. (*Matt Meuse-Dallien*)

a First Nation woman married a non-First Nation man, she was no longer allowed to identify as a First Nation person. She could not live on the reserve and had to move away. However, if a First Nation man married a non-First Nation woman, she was then considered First Nation, and lived on the reserve with her husband.

Since this rule was unfair to First Nation women, a new law (or bill) was passed in 1985 called Bill C-31.

L'nu'k: The People

Bands and Reserves by Province

Nova Scotia

Acadia
Gold River
Medway River
Ponhook Lake
Wildcat
Yarmouth

Annapolis Valley
Cambridge
St. Croix

Bear River
Bear River #6
Bear River #6A
Bear River #6B

Eskasoni
Malagawatch
Eskasoni #3
Eskasoni #3A

Glooscap First Nation
Horton

Membertou
Membertou
Caribou Marsh
Sydney
Malagawatch

Millbrook
Millbrook
Beaver Lake
Truro #27A
Truro #27B
Truro #27C
Cole Harbour
Sheet Harbour

Potlotek First Nation
Chapel Island
Malagawatch

Paq'tnkek
Franklin Manor
Pomquet & Afton
Summerside

Pictou Landing
Franklin Manor
Boat Harbour
Fisher's Grant #24
Fisher's Grant #24G
Merigomish Harbour

Sipenkne'katik
New Ross
Pennal
Shubenacadie
Indian Brook

Wagmatcook
Wagmatcook
Malagawatch
Margaree

Waycobah
Malagawatch
Whycocomagh
Buctouche

New Brunswick

Buctouche
Buctouche

Esgenoopetitj First Nation
Burnt Church
Tabusintac
Pokemouche

Eel Ground
Eel Ground
Big Hole Tract
Renous

Eel River Bar
Eel River Bar
Moose Meadows
Indian Ranch

Elsipogtog First Nation
Richibucto

Fort Folly
Fort Folly

Indian Island
Indian Island

Kingsclear (Maliseet)
Kingsclear
The Brothers
Oromocto

Madawaska Maliseet First Nation (Maliseet)
St. Basile
The Brothers

Metepenagiag Mi'kmaq Nation
Red Bank #4
Red Bank #7
Big Hole #8 North
Indian Point

Pabineau
Pabineau

Tobique (Maliseet)
Tobique
The Brothers

Woodstock (Maliseet)
Woodstock
The Brothers

St. Mary's (Maliseet)
Devon

Prince Edward Island

Abegweit
Morell
Rocky Point
Scrotchfort

Lennox Island
Lennox Island

Newfoundland & Labrador

Miawpukek
Samiajij Miawpukek

Qalipu Mi'kmaq First Nation

Quebec

La Nation Micmac de Gespeg

Listuguj Mi'gmaq Government

Micmacs of Gesgapegiag

Today, First Nation men and women can marry whomever they wish without it affecting their status identification with the government.

The way of life for First Nation people is still affected by government laws, but things are beginning to change for the better; First Nation leaders are now able to meet with all levels of government to help create positive change.

Modern Mi'kmaw Communities

Today, Mi'kmaw people live on and off reserves throughout Nova Scotia, New Brunswick, Prince Edward Island, and Newfoundland. There are others who live in Quebec, along the Gaspé, and in Maine, with some

Community buildings in Bear River, Nova Scotia. The red building on the left is a program or meeting space. The light-blue building on the right is the Bear River First Nation Band Hall, which has office space for the reserve's Band Council and its employees.

This cenotaph at Millbrook First Nation remembers Mi'kmaw soldiers who served their country.

others living throughout different parts of the world.

In Nova Scotia, there are thirteen Mi'kmaw bands and many of their membership live on forty-two separate reserve lands. The title "band" is given to a group of Mi'kmaq using a particular reserve land. For example: the Bear River Mi'kmaw Band uses three reserve lands which are located in Bear River, Lequille, and Graywood. The Millbrook Mi'kmaw Band uses four reserve lands located in Truro, Cole Harbour, Sheet Harbour, and Beaver Dam.

COMMUNITY LIFE

As part of the Indian Act, each First Nation must have an on-reserve government. This individual government is known as a band council and is made up of one chief and several councillors who serve as the leaders of the community (the exact number depends on each band's population). The band council approves developments

More buildings on the Bear River Reserve. The red-and-white building on the left is a preschool, which also provides after-school programs. The smaller building on the right is a bus shelter.

taking place on the reserve, such as construction, school systems, and health services. Each band's membership votes for the band members they want to represent them in the council.

Elections are held at least every two years, although there is a system in place to change this to four years. (Some bands have already changed their election schedule.) All band members are identified by a specific number whether they live on- or off-reserve. As long as they are at least eighteen years old, members can vote in these elections.

Each band has offices where band council members discuss community issues such as economic development, which involves building gas stations, stores, or cultural centres; education, which involves working to have preschool and higher levels of education delivered in the community; and social programs, which help their members live better and provide for different types of housing.

There are also health centres in each community that provide health programs like diabetes clinics, nutrition classes, and doctors' appointments. Some bands may have schools, churches, stores, community centres, and other businesses depending on the location and size of the reserve.

A lot has changed for the Mi'kmaq in recent years, and their communities continue to grow.

CHAPTER 3

Spirituality Connections

For many Mi'kmaq, everyday life has a spiritual connection. Whether fishing, hunting, storytelling, healing, or celebrating, we always make time to show gratitude and respect to Kisu'lkw, the Creator, for the things Mother Earth provides: food, water, land, and, of course, us. Spirituality is very important to the Mi'kmaq, although these days other forms of prayer and offering

What is Healing?

Healing is something you do to try to make yourself feel better. It is more than physically healing from an illness: it means trying to have good mental and spiritual health along with helping to look after the environment that surrounds us.

Healing can be done through praying, resting, reading, exercising, talking, writing, or even just walking. Helping to keep the forests healthy, the water clean, and the lands protected from pollution and destruction is also beneficial for spiritual healing. Often, it's something you need to do more than once.

Healing is not just a goal, it is a process that requires time and effort.

thanks are practiced in addition to the following cultural teachings.

You will notice some pictures in this chapter are photos and others are paintings or drawings. My Elders have taught me not to use actual photographs of our sacred ceremonies like the sweat lodge, sacred fire, or smudging. This is because a lot of our cultural practices have been lost over the years, and our ceremonies are not meant to be on display or treated like entertainment. Some traditions have been disrespected (even in today's society), so we must try to keep sacred what we can. The Elders further teach that the best way to learn about these things is to visit a First Nation community and actively participate in a ceremony.

Mother Earth

The First Nation people use the English words "Mother Earth" to describe the Earth that was made by Kisu'lkw. Just like a human mother gives life to her baby, Mother Earth gives life to the trees, plants, rocks, animals, water, air, and all other things that help humans live here.

All these things are important to our health. That is why we must learn to respect Mother Earth by helping to keep the air, water, and lands clean. Some good practices to help protect Mother Earth are to throw trash in the garbage bin, recycle bottles and plastics, and compost leftover food.

What other things can you do to help protect Mother Earth?

Spirituality

Like most First Nation beliefs, Mi'kmaw spirituality includes all things Kisu'lkw provides. It recognizes the spirit within every natural thing on Earth: humans, animals, plants, forests, rocks, lakes, rivers, and oceans. The Mi'kmaq know the spirits within these things are a lot like the spirits within us and must be treated with honour and respect. In practice, this means not harming animals needlessly. If an animal needs to be killed for food or clothing, you should always give thanks to its spirit for sacrificing its life. The same holds true for trees, flowers, plants, and all other things provided by the Creator. The simple idea is: try not to take anything you don't need, don't waste what you do take, and always offer thanks. Sometimes, this is done by leaving tobacco.

Ceremonial tobacco is grown specifically to use in Mi'kmaw ceremonies. Grown in a natural way (without added chemicals or other types of processing), it is the preferred tobacco to use as one of the four sacred medicines.

Some First Nation people may have different names for Kisu'lkw, the Creator: God, Great Spirit, Higher Being, or another name depending on their personal belief.

"Oh, Great Spirit" Prayer

Prayer time in First Nation culture is very important and occurs during ceremonies. Although there are all types of prayers for healing, wisdom, and guidance, this is one of the favourite prayers recited by many First Nation people, including the Mi'kmaq:

Oh, Great Spirit, whose voice I hear in the wind,
hear me for I am young, small, and weak.
I need your strength, Oh Great One, not to be superior to my
    Brothers and Sisters,
but to conquer my greatest enemy: myself.
I seek wisdom, the lessons you have hidden in every leaf and rock,
so that I may carry this message of life and hope to my people.
May my hands respect the many beautiful things you have made.
May my ears be sharp to hear your voice.
May I always walk in your beauty and let my eyes ever behold the
    red and purple sunset.
So that when life fades like the setting sun, my Spirit will come to
    you without shame.

Written by a respected First Nation Elder (some versions say Lakota Chief Yellow Lark, 1887)

Some Mi'kmaw people may also have another belief that helps direct them through life.

In this book, the term Kisu'lkw will be used to help explain our spiritual connection to Mother Earth. Although there are several branches of spirituality practiced today, the two main practises of the Mi'kmaq are: our cultural teachings and the Roman Catholic

Spirituality Connections

religion. Cultural teachings include understanding how Mother Earth works and our connection to her well-being. Ceremonies, stories, and prayers are used to help people understand and learn these teachings.

Elders

"Elder" is the respectful name given to an older person within the Mi'kmaw community. Elders are respected for their knowledge and wisdom and are asked to help with community activities, ceremonies, and may be asked to help make important decisions within a community. They may lead ceremonies (such as smudging ceremonies and talking circles) and share their vast knowledge, history, and stories with everyone. Elders should be respected, and others should help and care for them at all times.

There is no set age when one is considered an Elder but they are usually older, because it takes many years to gain knowledge and wisdom. A person may have several different Elders they speak with depending on what they want to talk about. For example, a female may go to a female Elder for certain guidance, and male Elders for other teachings.

Sacred Medicines and the Smudging Ceremony

Unlit braided sweetgrass, a sacred medicine used in smudging ceremonies.

Sacred medicines—also know as sacred herbs—include four main medicines: sweetgrass, to cleanse the body, mind, and spirit; sage, to help get rid of negativity; cedar, a protector throughout a person's life; and ceremonial tobacco, offered as thanks to Kisu'lkw.

Medicines can be sprinkled about the ground or burned in a bowl or shell, both are known as an offering. When the medicines are lit during prayer time, it is called a "smudging ceremony" and is always led by an Elder or adult. During a smudging ceremony, the smoke from the burning medicines is directed to seven distinct parts of the body: to the eyes, to help see the good in other people; to the ears, to help hear and listen to others; to the mouth, so only good words are spoken; to the mind, so we have good thoughts; to the feet, so good paths are followed throughout life; to the whole body,

Smudge Bowl

A smudge bowl can be a large shell, stone, or clay bowl used to burn sacred medicines during a smudging ceremony.

Spiritual leaders may mix one or more sacred medicines together in the smudge bowl, allowing them to burn for a longer period of time.

The most common material used for a smudge bowl is an abalone shell because its large size and thickness prevents the holder from getting hurt while the medicines are burned.

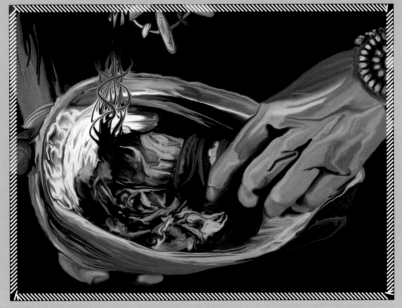

A beautiful painting showing the sacred medicines burning in an abalone-shell smudge bowl. (*Gerald Gloade*)

to have respect for the self; and lastly, to the heart, so it remains pure and respects all Creation. Anyone can take part in a smudging ceremony. It can be done at any time of the day or night and as often as necessary. Respect should be shown at all times during the ceremony.

L'nu'k: The People

Medicine Wheel

Some believe the medicine wheel was not part of the traditional Mi'kmaw teachings and consider it a borrowed teaching from the western First Nation people. Despite this belief, I have been taught that the Mi'kmaq live in harmony with nature and man and the medicine wheel is one example of how we can uphold that way of life. It is viewed as "a" way, not "the" way.

The medicine wheel is the same shape as a dream catcher but does not have the web weaved in the middle. Instead, there are four strips of leather attached to the circle, representing the four directions (east, south, west and north). You will notice that the order in which the directions are written may be different from what you're used to. Instead of north, south, east, then west, First Nation teachings begin with east, and proceed clockwise from there: south, west, then north. Each direction of the medicine wheel includes teachings that change depending on how a person wishes to use them in their life's journey.

The colours of the medicine wheel can mean different things, and many people like to use red, white, yellow, and black to represent four races of the world. In this

A MEDICINE WHEEL EXAMPLE:
GIFTS FROM THE DIRECTIONS

NORTH
Mental
Elder
Winter
Water
Black
Tobacco
Turtle
Lily of the valley
Pine

WEST
Physical
Adult
Autumn
Fire
Red
Sage
Spider
Buttercup
Birch

EAST (START)
Spiritual
Child
Spring
Air
White
Sweetgrass
Eagle
Lilac
Ash

SOUTH
Environmental
Adolescent
Summer
Soil
Yellow
Cedar
Ladybug
Black-Eyed Susan
Maple

L'nu'k: The People

example, the colours in my medicine wheel represent a whole day: white in the east to represent the hours before sunrise (dawn); yellow in the south for the hours after the sun rises (daytime); red in the west for the setting sun (dusk); and black in the north after the sun goes down (dark). This reminds me that my life's journey continues all day every day, even when I'm sleeping.

Although there are many teachings of the medicine wheel, its main purpose is to remind us to take good care of ourselves. The following is one example: From the east direction, we are reminded to be thankful to Kisu'lkw for life, known as our spiritual well-being; the south direction reminds us to help take care of everything Mother Earth provides, known as our environmental well-being; the west direction reminds us to keep our body healthy, known as our physical well-being; and the north direction reminds us to try and have happy thoughts, known as our mental well-being.

Each direction also describes a stage of life—east is childhood (spring), south is adolescence (summer), west is adulthood (autumn), and north is Elder (winter). The directions on the medicine wheel can also represent the four sacred medicines, animals, trees, flowers, elements, and many other things.

Spirituality Connections

Other teachings and gifts from Kisu'lkw can be added to the directions depending on personal choice. Some may include sacred teachings like, "in the east comes truth; south, trust; west, patience; north, wisdom." It is your medicine wheel—your life's journey—so it is up to you to decide the teachings you will take along with you.

Sacred Items

EAGLE FEATHER

The Mi'kmaq consider the eagle, known for its skilful flying and hunting, the most powerful bird in the sky. It is believed that of all the birds, the eagle gets the closest to the Kisu'lkw and helps carry our prayers to the spirit world.

When collecting feathers, eagles are not to be harmed in any way. Some feathers can be found naturally in the woods, some are given as gifts, and most are provided by Natural Resources Canada, whose workers collect them from national parks and forests.

An eagle feather, sometimes used during prayer time.

L'nu'k: The People

A Dream Catcher Story

There are many stories written about how the dream catcher came to be; this is one of them.

A spider started to make its web near the window of an Elder's home. For several days, the Elder watched the spider weave until its web was big enough to catch food. One day, the Elder's grandson came to visit and she showed him the web. The grandson wanted to destroy the web and kill the spider but the Elder told him not to harm either.

Soon after the grandson left, the Elder went back to check on the spider and its web. The spider then spoke to the Elder and thanked her for saving his life. In gratitude, the spider wanted to give her a gift. The spider taught her how to weave a web like his. He called it a dream catcher and told her it would help her always have good dreams: the web would snare bad dreams and only let good ones pass through the hole in the middle.

The Elder learned to weave a dream catcher and then decorated it with leather, feathers, and beads. The Elder taught others how to make the dream catcher to make sure everyone would have good dreams throughout life. -Author Unknown

Being presented with an eagle feather is a great honour. It is given to someone to recognize a good deed they have done or for showing knowledge in their cultural teachings. You should never touch another person's eagle feather (or any of their spiritual medicines explained in this chapter) without permission. To do so is seen as disrespectful.

DREAM CATCHER

An example of a dream catcher.

Some people believe dream catchers did not originate with the Mi'kmaq, but Mi'kmaw people have been creating this art for a very long time.

Dream catchers are round hoops with what looks like a spider's web in the middle. According to legends and stories, dream catchers trap bad dreams in their webs and only allow good dreams to filter through a hole in the centre. Some First Nation people hang them above their beds or in other places throughout their home.

The web of a dream catcher is traditionally made from animal sinew, but string, dental floss, or thread can also be used. The webbing and hoops can be decorated with beads, feathers, or pieces of leather. Dream catchers can be different sizes and colours depending on individual preference.

MEDICINE BUNDLE

A medicine bundle is used for carrying different items that help create a spiritual connection to Kisu'lkw, like an eagle feather, smudge bowl, sacred medicines, animal claws or teeth, a sacred pipe, and/or a hand drum—all things used during sacred ceremonies.

A medicine bundle may start out as a small bag and change in size depending on the number of things collected throughout one's life. Sometimes, the items are gifts from a ceremony or celebration, and sometimes they are simply items the individual has collected. Like all sacred medicines, bundles are kept in a private place and only brought out during ceremonial times.

MEDICINE POUCH

The medicine pouch—also known as a medicine bag or offering bag—is used to carry smaller things, like sacred medicines, stones, feathers, shells, or something that belonged to a loved one; anything that provides personal healing or protection to the wearer. The medicine inside the pouch can be used for healing of the self or others, worn upon the death of a love one, used as a reminder of their connection to the Creator, or possibly in memory of someone. The medicines are totally unique

Medicine Plants in Your Backyard

Many traditional Mi'kmaw medicine plants are still available today as well as some newer ones. For many people, the newer medicines are now considered weeds and destroyed with sprays or other toxic chemicals. The following are a few of the more common plants you might be able to find in your own backyard and their medicinal uses. Remember: you should never take medicine without asking an expert.

Dandelion: Both the flower and the leaves have medicinal value. The leaves, when steeped in hot water, act as a diuretic (increasing the amount of urine to help clean your kidneys). The flower, when prepared the same way, is an antioxidant (which helps your immune system fight disease).

Buttercup: The scent (or juice) of the leaves, when applied directly to the nostrils, is said to cure headaches. Be careful, though: the juice can cause blisters if you use too much!

Red clover (burdock): The roots can be steeped in hot water and consumed two or three times a day to purify the blood. The blossoms, when steeped, are used to control high fevers.

Plantain: The leaves can be ground up (or chewed) to create a paste that, when applied directly to a sore or an insect bite or sting, can help draw out the venom or poison. The whole leaves can also be steeped in hot water to make a tea that is used to treat stomach ulcers.

Wild strawberry: Chew or steep the leaves of a wild strawberry plant to treat stomach cramps or infections in the intestines. A strong tea made of the roots, leaves, and berries can be gargled to clean and strengthen the gums.

Blackberry: The entire plant can be used to treat diarrhea, but the roots and leaves, when steeped and drank as tea, are the best (just remember to remove the thorns!). A tea made from the berries is good for treating canker sores in the mouth or throat.

Example of some medicine pouch designs.

to the individual and can be worn any time they are needed around the neck, on a belt, or carried within the medicine bundle.

Traditional Medicine Plants

Many Mi'kmaq have always had great knowledge about the plants and animals living around them and how to harvest them for medicine to prevent and cure many illnesses. For example, they knew eel oil was good for earaches, and bone marrow (taken from the shin bone of a moose) when rubbed onto hands or knees, helped ease arthritis pain.

Hundreds of years ago, when someone was sick or injured, the Mi'kmaq looked to a medicine person for guidance, much like we look to a modern doctor. Someone could become a medicine person by learning from Elders which plants did what, how to harvest them, and how to prepare the medicines. Since every patient was different, the medicine person needed to know how to prepare the ingredients based on the patient's symptoms, age, height, and weight.

Sacred Ceremonies

TALKING CIRCLE

The talking circle is a respectful way to communicate within a group and can last for many hours. An Elder will usually begin the talking circle with a prayer and smudging ceremony. Everyone sits in a circle and the Elder, while holding the talking stick, will be the first to speak. The Elder may share anything—a story, a memory, a prayer—and then pass the talking stick (or another item, like an eagle feather) to the person on their left. Whoever holds the talking stick is the only person allowed to speak; everyone must listen and wait their turn.

The talking stick may go around the circle many times. The circle is only considered over when the stick has made one complete circle without anyone speaking. When people are part of a circle that has a time limit or only allows for people to have one turn holding the talking stick, it is known as a "sharing circle." If you know you might have to leave a circle before it is completed, speak to the Elder before the circle starts.

Two different talking sticks that might be used during a talking circle.

Other types of circles can include: healing, justice, sentencing, or community. Circle discussions can be on many different topics or focus on just one. The Elder or leader (and sometimes the group as a whole) will select the topic or topics. Circles can be held indoors or outdoors but should always be held in a private area where there is little noise and distraction.

Although it rarely happens, if someone shows disrespect during a talking circle, the leader could be forced to excuse that person or ask the circle to stop.

Trust is very important during a circle. The things people share can be very private or personal and it is disrespectful to tell other people what someone has shared. A common phrase you will hear in a talking circle is, "what gets said in the circle remains in the circle." Some people may cry or have strong emotions.

Question: Besides listening and not interrupting, what would be some other ways to show respect during a talking circle?

Answer: Do not make fun of people or laugh at what a person chooses to talk about, do not use cellphones or other electronics, do not use bad language, do not call others names, and be gentle when passing the talking stick.

It is okay to show feelings, and if it happens, just sit quietly and wait for the person to begin talking again or pass on the stick. Other times, there may be laughter because some people like to share funny stories. All circles can be a healing time for everyone involved.

SWEAT LODGE

A sweat lodge is a dome-shaped structure—much like a wigwam, except with a rounded roof. A sweat lodge ceremony involves several people gathering together in a sweat lodge to pray to Kisu'lkw for healing, teachings, and guidance. An Elder will guide everyone before, during, and after a ceremony.

Sweat lodge ceremonies can be different each time; one Elder may smudge, pray, sing, chant, or drum differently from another.

After everyone has entered the sweat lodge, hot stones are brought in by the fire

An example of what a sweat lodge and sacred fire might look like all set up.

Grandmother and Grandfather Stones

Stones are used in ceremonies such as the talking circle, sacred fires, and sweat lodges. Stones are seen as the oldest thing on Mother Earth and therefore they hold the most history. They are called the Grandfathers and Grandmothers in respect of all ancestors who have lived on Mother Earth since the beginning of time. Many First Nation people believe that when the stones are heated, they release the teachings of the Ancestors.

keeper, and placed in a pit at the centre. These stones, known as Grandfathers and Grandmothers, are heated in the fire before the ceremony begins. Once everyone is seated and the Grandmothers and Grandfathers are placed, the door of the lodge is closed and the sweat lodge ceremony begins.

Part of the ceremony involves sprinkling water on the heated stones to create steam, which makes the sweat lodge feel much like a sauna. As the steam fills the lodge, it helps to cleanse the mind, body, and spirit, and everyone can pray.

Every sweat lodge ceremony is different; the sweat lodge keeper may lead everyone in prayer, there may also be singing, chanting, or drumming. (The sweat lodge keeper is someone who has earned the privilege to take care of a sweat lodge and lead a ceremony by learning and practicing the traditional teachings under the direction of an Elder). The ceremony can last for a long time—some last several hours!—and varies depending on the number of people in the lodge. Some will go into a sweat lodge on a regular basis; others will go once a week or a few times a year.

A sweat lodge can take place any time throughout the year. The keeper of the sweat lodge is responsible for the lodge all year long and helps to get it ready for use. By learning and practicing traditional teachings under the direction of an Elder, a sweat lodge keeper is someone who has earned the privilege to take care of the lodge and also lead the ceremony if the Elder is unavailable.

There are also sweat lodge ceremonies just for men, just for women, and ceremonies called "mixed sweats," where both men and women participate. Children can also go into a sweat lodge as long as they have a parent's permission.

SACRED FIRE

The sacred fire is normally burned for four days and four nights but in some cases it might be less: one-day fires are very popular. Shorter fires may be burned for a special person or situation. For example, a fire may be lit the same day someone is having surgery.

The sacred fire is also used during sweat lodge ceremonies to heat the Grandfather and Grandmother stones. It is a time for people to pray for healing and to give thanks to Kisu'lkw for all that Mother Earth provides. People will sprinkle sacred medicines—like sage, sweetgrass, cedar and/or ceremonial tobacco—onto the fire as an offering and say a silent prayer. The smoke helps take the prayers to Kisu'lkw. Others like to sit around the sacred fire to mediate or be part of a talking circle. Before the fire is lit, a fire keeper will prepare the grounds and hold ceremonies that vary depending on the Elder. When the fire is lit, fire keepers are always available, day and night, to help teach others about the sacred fire. People can stay at the fire as long as they like and usually make offerings in the morning and at night.

SACRED PIPE

There are different types of sacred pipes, but the most common are the individual and community pipes. Some First Nation people may call it a "peace pipe" but the common Mi'kmaw name is the "sacred pipe." It is a privilege to have a sacred pipe, and traditionally, you will only receive one if an Elder feels you are ready. An individual pipe is one a person uses just for his or her personal use. A community pipe, kept safe by a pipe keeper, is used during a ceremony involving many people.

Depending on the Elder, a pipe ceremony may include smudging, prayer time, drumming, and/or singing. Normally ceremonial tobacco, which is specially grown for this purpose, is used in the pipe. The Elder will light the pipe and then pass it to the person on their left. Each person standing in the circle gets to hold the pipe and puff on it if they wish to, though they do not normally inhale the smoke; many prefer to just hold the pipe while they say their prayer. Children are encouraged to be part of the ceremony but are not permitted to smoke the pipe. They will just hold the pipe respectfully during their prayer time. The Elder will guide everyone during the ceremony. It is a sign of friendship and respect to be invited to take part in a sacred pipe ceremony.

Musical Instruments

DRUMS

First Nation people know the sound of a drum is the heartbeat of Mother Earth. Just like a baby can hear the heartbeat of its mother, when we hear the beat of the drum it reminds us to be kind to each other and to the Earth.

There are two types of drums: the individual, smaller hand drum, and the big, round "group" drum. The hand drum is smaller and fits into a person's hand, is usually round, and sometimes has a painting on its surface. The round or group drum is about 1 metre in diameter and sits on a drum stand placed on the ground while it is played by a group. Usually the group is mainly male, but there are some female drum groups as well. Drumming can take place at any time, but mostly occurs during ceremonies.

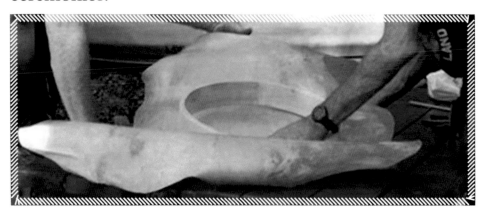

Stretching the animal skin to be made into a small hand drum.

L'nu'k: The People

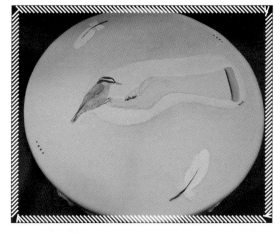

Top and bottom of a small hand drum. Not all drums are decorated, but each one is crafted the same way.

In Mi'kma'ki, drums are made from materials gathered from Mother Earth: wood from the spruce or cedar tree and leather made from deer or moose hide. Once the wood is bent into a round shape, the leather is stretched across it and attached using lacing made from the hide. No nails, screws, or other metals are used to put the drums together.

Drumsticks are usually made using the leftover wood, with leather or softer material attached to one end to serve as the pounding end. There are several Mi'kmaw drum makers; traditionally they determine when it is time for a person to receive the gift of a drum. There are, however, group workshops conducted where everyone gets to make a drum. Like with all medicines, respect for a Mi'kmaw drum must be shown at all times. To show disrespect could cause a drum to break or be taken back by the Elder.

Just like the ash baskets, Mi'kmaw drums are very sturdy and can last for many years.

JI'KMAQN: THE CHANTING STICK

The *ji'kmaqn* (jig-gah-mah-hun), or "chanting stick," is a wooden musical instrument played during drumming and singing time. It is also made from ash, and the preparation is similar to that of weaving a basket. The length of the stick, however, is much smaller than that of the wood used for making baskets (about 1 foot long) and only one end of the stick gets pounded until the growth rings start to separate. The stick is sometimes decorated with paint or leather, but some prefer to keep theirs natural.

Stages of creating a *ji'kmaqn*. Similar stages are used for making basket splints.

To play the chanting stick, the player holds the non-pounded end—the handle—and, slapping

L'nu'k: The People

the separated end into the palm of his or her other hand, keeps beat to the music. Sometimes, a person will carry a *ji'kmaqn* in their medicine bundle.

Dancing

Like many people, the Mi'kmaq have a special way of dancing that is unique. Traditional Mi'kmaw dancing is a celebration of life, and each dance tells a story. Some group dances mimic the movements of animals, like in the snake dance: dancers line up, touch the shoulders of the person in front of them, and follow the leader

The beautiful colours (white, yellow, red, and black of the medicine wheel) and design of regalia worn at a public powwow in Halifax in 2010. (*Lynda Mallett*)

Spirituality Connections

who weaves in and out, trying to recreate the coiling movement of a snake. Some dances use swooping movements and sounds to mimic birds. Other group dances include the round dance, where everyone holds hands and dances in a circle.

There are many different individual dances too: the jingle dance features girls' regalia decorated to give off a jingling sound when they move; shawl dances involve the females moving their shawls over their shoulders like butterflies; and the grass dance is a symbolic male dance that prepares the land for other dances to take place. Many Mi'kmaq start dancing at a young age and continue their whole lives.

Regalia

Most traditional dancers wear beautifully crafted regalia made especially for them. All regalia are unique and tell a story of the wearer's dancing journey. Their designs can include beads, feathers, ribbons, or other items to express the dancers' personal history.

Regalia are *not* costumes; they are spiritual connections to Kisu'lkw and are worn to show respect during ceremonies. Since regalia are so special, it is very

The Lucio family of Indian Brook First Nation taking a break from dancing to show their regalia. (*Master Corporal Vincent Carbonneau*)

disrespectful to the First Nation culture to dress up in or try to imitate the First Nation regalia as a Halloween costume. Taking items from another culture and wearing or using them for fun disrespects their special meaning and importance. This is known as "cultural appropriation." You should also not touch regalia without permission from its owner.

Powwow

A modern-day powwow is usually a two-day event held over a weekend that anyone can attend to learn about First Nation culture. It can include some of the ceremonies—like a sacred fire and smudging—but there are also booths for people to sell crafts and food, or to put on craft-making demonstrations, and dancing and drumming competitions. It is a time for celebrating First Nation culture.

A painting by Mi'kmaw artist Brianne Zee showing powwow grounds set up with an arbor for hosting drum groups. People will dance outside the arbor.

L'nu'k: The People

Everyone is welcome to attend the celebration, but alcohol and drugs are not permitted at the powwow. Some powwows will permit dogs on leashes, but it is always a good idea to get permission before bringing your pet. You should also get permission before taking pictures and videos at a powwow.

Mawiomi

Mawiomi (maow-ee-oh-mee) is a Mi'kmaw word meaning "gathering." This is a cultural get-together to celebrate life. Some Elders teach that a traditional mawiomi would have once lasted up to four days and included ceremonies and activities like sweat lodges, sacred fires, games of waltes, storytelling, talking circles, drumming, crafting, dancing, singing, and feasting.

Today, some Mi'kmaw people will refer to a powwow as a "mawiomi" or "gathering." Although similar, the activities at a modern powwow vary depending on the host community.

People from all cultures are invited to attend a powwow or *mawiomi*, making it a social time with feasting and gathering for self-healing or spiritual connection. Some Mi'kmaq will host a *mawiomi* with no vendors or competitions or pets allowed. These gatherings are not normally advertised.

Whether a *mawiomi* or powwow, each celebration offers unique ways to learn about Mi'kmaw culture.

Keep Learning!

From reading this book, I hope you have learned something new and are inspired to keep learning more. The best way to learn about the Mi'kmaq or other First Nation people is to visit a community near you, especially one that has a cultural or visitor's centre. Also, make sure to check out the websites, books, and museums listed on pages 111 to 113 for more information.

Nova Scotia Mi'kmaw Firsts

1874 Gabriel J. Sylliboy of Whycocomagh is *elected* Grand Chief. Before this, the Grand Chief role was hereditary, meaning it was passed down from father to son.

1937 Elsie Basque of Digby County becomes the first licensed Mi'kmaw teacher in Nova Scotia.

1978 Rita Joe becomes the first Mi'kmaw author to publish a book of poems.

1980 The Smith-Francis Orthography becomes the official spelling system of the Mi'kmaw written language.

1989 Rita Joe is awarded the Order of Canada, a prestigious award established by Queen Elizabeth II to recognize outstanding achievement, dedication, and service.

1992 Eleanor Johnson of Eskasoni becomes the first person to write a Masters thesis entirely in the Mi'kmaw language (Department of Anthropology, Saint Mary's University).

1993 Adam Gould of Membertou becomes the first student to receive first place in the Sammy Gehue Achievement Awards. The Awards were established in 1993 to honour and remember Sammy Gehue, a Mi'kmaw child from Indian Brook who showed great determination and strength despite an illness that took his life at age seven. Today, the award annually recognizes three Mi'kmaw students for their achievements in academic, cultural, and humanitarian learning.

1994 Daniel N. Paul becomes the first Mi'kmaw Justice of the Peace, allowing him to perform weddings, issue summons and subpoenas (for court), and administer oaths.

1996 Lee Cremo becomes the first Mi'kmaq to win an East Coast Music Award, Best First Nation Recording for his fiddle music.

1996 Robert Johnson of Millbrook is awarded the National Aboriginal Achievement Award. Two years later, he graduates as a medical doctor from Dalhousie University, the first Mi'kmaw of Nova Scotia to do so.

2000 Noel Knockwood of Indian Brook becomes the first Mi'kmaw Sergeant-at-Arms of the Nova Scotia House of Assembly.

2001 Cathy Martin of Millbrook wins the Andres Slapinsh International Award for Best Indigenous Filmmaker for her film *Spirit Wind*.

2016 Mi'kmaw spoken word artist Rebecca Thomas becomes Halifax Regional Municipality's Poet Laureate, Canada's first First Nation poet to hold the honour.

2016 Danny Christmas of Membertou First Nation in Cape Breton becomes Canada's first Mi'kmaw senator.

2017 Gerald Gloade, a Mi'kmaw artist from Millbrook First Nation, becomes the first Mi'kmaq to have artwork featured (a beaver design) on the Canadian nickel.

Mi'kmaw Historical Timeline

1507   Grand Chief Membertou is born.

1610   Grand Chief Membertou is the first Mi'kmaq to be baptized in the Roman Catholic religion, at Annapolis Royal in Nova Scotia.

1700   Many Mi'kmaw treaties signed with the British government.

1801   First eleven Mi'kmaw reserves established in Nova Scotia.

1876   The Canadian government passes the Indian Act.

1914   Approximately 150 Mi'kmaw men sign up to fight in the First World War.

1930   The only residential school in Atlantic Canada opens, in Shubenacadie, Nova Scotia.

1939   Over 250 Mi'kmaw men sign up to fight in the Second World War.

1942   The Canadian government proposes its centralization policy. All Mi'kmaw people in Nova Scotia are told to live in either Shubenacadie or Eskasoni, and Tobique or Big Cove in New Brunswick.

1950	Over 60 Mi'kmaw men sign up to fight in the Korean War.
1951	Once banned in the Indian Act, the government changes its policy and allows First Nation people to openly practice their spiritual ceremonies.
1956	The federal government officially recognizes First Nation people as Canadian citizens.
1960	First Nation people are allowed to vote in the provincial and federal elections.
1969	Union of Nova Scotia Indians (UNSI) is formed. Located in Cape Breton, UNSI is a tribal council that provides services to its members' bands.
1972	The Micmac Association of Cultural Studies is formed in Cape Breton to help promote Mi'kmaw culture.
1972	The Nova Scotia Native Women's Association is formed at Millbrook; the organization provides services to Native women in areas of education, technical training, and job opportunities.
1973	A twelfth First Nation band is established: Acadia First Nation in Yarmouth, Nova Scotia.
1973	The Mi'kmaw Native Friendship Centre is established in Halifax. This organization provides assistance and services for urban Aboriginal people in areas of education, employment, culture, and more.

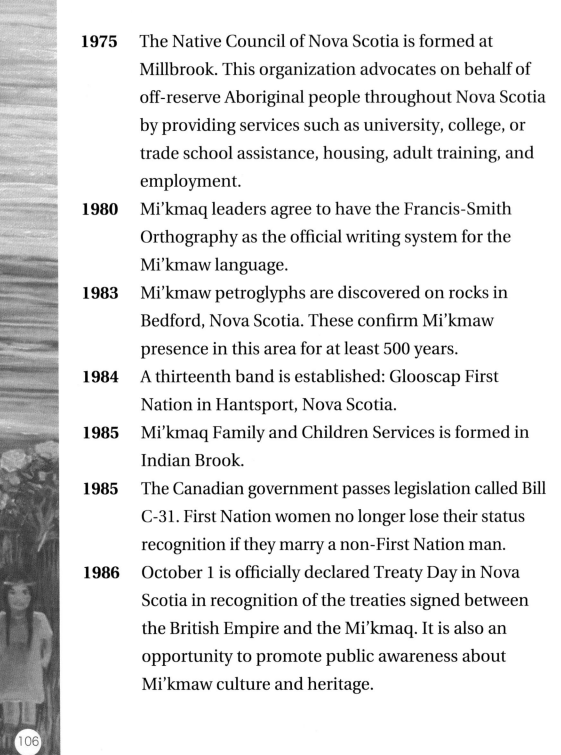

1975 The Native Council of Nova Scotia is formed at Millbrook. This organization advocates on behalf of off-reserve Aboriginal people throughout Nova Scotia by providing services such as university, college, or trade school assistance, housing, adult training, and employment.

1980 Mi'kmaq leaders agree to have the Francis-Smith Orthography as the official writing system for the Mi'kmaw language.

1983 Mi'kmaw petroglyphs are discovered on rocks in Bedford, Nova Scotia. These confirm Mi'kmaw presence in this area for at least 500 years.

1984 A thirteenth band is established: Glooscap First Nation in Hantsport, Nova Scotia.

1985 Mi'kmaq Family and Children Services is formed in Indian Brook.

1985 The Canadian government passes legislation called Bill C-31. First Nation women no longer lose their status recognition if they marry a non-First Nation man.

1986 October 1 is officially declared Treaty Day in Nova Scotia in recognition of the treaties signed between the British Empire and the Mi'kmaq. It is also an opportunity to promote public awareness about Mi'kmaw culture and heritage.

1986 The Confederacy of Mainland Mi'kmaq is formed in Truro, Nova Scotia. Known as Tribal Council, this organization provides services to its members' bands in areas of post-secondary education support, forestry management, economic development, and health promotion.

1989 Dalhousie University establishes the Dalhousie Law School Program for Indigenous Black and Mi'kmaw students.

1990 *Micmac Nations News*, a First Nation–owned community newspaper, is established. Today, it is called the *Mi'kmaq-Maliseet Nations News* and is circulated monthly.

1995 The Atlantic Policy Congress of First Nation Chiefs is established in Dartmouth, Nova Scotia.

1999 Atlantic Canada's First Nation Help Desk is formed to help students and teachers develop high-tech support for First Nation schools.

2000 A historic plaque and monument is established at Kejimkujik National Park and National Historic Site in recognition of the Mi'kmaw people.

2000 The Dalhousie University's Transitional Year Program is established for Aboriginal students.

2008 Prime Minister Stephen Harper makes a public apology to the residential school survivors and their families for the hardships they suffered as a result of the residential school system.

2008 The federal government establishes a Truth and Reconciliation Commission to research and make public the negative impacts of the residential school system.

2011 *Qalipu* (ha-lee-pu) Mi'kmaq Band is established in Newfoundland. The *Qalipu* Band has over 24,000 members but does not have reserve land.

2015 The Truth and Reconciliation Commission releases its final report, recommending developments for First Nation people and communities in areas of child welfare, education, language, culture, health, and justice.

2016 A national inquiry is started to find out why so many First Nation women go missing or are murdered across Canada.

L'nu'k: The People

Acknowledgements

This book would not have been possible without the help of some amazing people. I wish to acknowledge each person who willingly answered my many questions, gave positive guidance, or shared their wonderful pictures: *wela'lioq* for your contributions and kindness.

My gratitude to: Frank Meuse, for sharing his knowledge of the forest and his pictures; Todd Labrador, for his photos and knowledge of the canoe, drums, and birchbark teachings; Bernie Francis, for giving us the written Mi'kmaw language, and to Bernie and Trudy Sable for helping identify its proper usage throughout this book; Elder Daniel N. Paul, for his historical knowledge; Gerald Gloade, for his beautiful artwork and traditional knowledge; Rose Meuse, for helping identify grammatical spelling of Mi'kmaw words; Laurie Lacey, for his knowledge of Mi'kmaw medicines; Darlene Ricker, for her historical information; Shalan Joudry, for graciously contributing her knowledge of our traditional culture; Roger Lewis, for giving me lots of amazing pictures and historical information; Bonnie Labrador, for some wonderful pictures; Mike Issac, for his cultural and historical knowledge; Donna Morris, for her understanding of our traditional culture and history; Leland Surette, for sharing his cultural teachings; Dusty Meuse, for his knowledge of traditional flowers, and to Matthew Meuse-Dallien, for the great map and legend of the Maritimes he created just for this book. Thank you also to Alan Syliboy for sharing his teachings.

Last but not least, a thank you to Nimbus Publishing for taking on this project, and to Emily MacKinnon for her editing expertise.

Special thanks to: my husband, Kevin Dallien; my daughters, Kerry (Shawn) and Tammy (Richard), and my son, Matthew; my grandchildren, Alex, Hunter, Rachael, and Warren; my siblings, Frank, Steve, Rosie, Dusty, and their families. Thank you all for your never-ending support and encouragement. So happy we are family!

Kesiluk.

Resources

Children's Books

How The Cougar Came To Be Called The Ghost Cat and *The Lost Teachings* (written in Mi'kmaw and English) by Michael James Isaac, illustrated by Dozay Christmas

The Sharing Circle by Theresa Meuse-Dallien

The Thundermaker by Alan Syliboy

Weska'qelmut Apje'juanu by Sheree Fitch, translated by Bernie Francis

General Books

Clay Pots and Bones by Lindsay Marshall

Generations Re-merging by Shalan Joudry

Mi'kmaq Anthology edited by Rita Joe and Lesley Choyce

Mi'kmaq Anthology, Volume 2 by Theresa Meuse, Lesley Choyce, and Julia Swan

Mi'kmaq Medicines: Remedies and Recollections (Second Edition) by Laurie Lacey

Mi'kmawe'l Tan Teli-kina'muemk: Teaching about the Mi'kmaq by the Confederacy of Mainland Mi'kmaq and the Mi'kmawey Debert Cultural Centre

Ni'n na L'nu: The Mi'kmaq of Prince Edward Island by Jesse Francis and A. J. B. Johnston

Out of the Depths: The Experiences of Mi'kmaw Children at the Indian Residential School at Shubenacadie, Nova Scotia by Isabelle Knockwood

Song of Rita Joe, We are the Dreamers, and *Lnu and Indians We're Called* all by Rita Joe

The Language of this Land, Mi'kma'ki by Trudy Sable and Bernie Francis

We Were Not the Savages (Third Edition) by Daniel N. Paul

Websites

Atlantic Canada's First Nation Help Desk: firstnationhelp.com

Atlantic Native Organization: apcfnc.ca

Alan Syliboy (Mi'kmaw artist, author): alansyliboy.com

Daniel Paul (Mi'kmaw historian, author): danielnpaul.com

General First Nation Cultural Awareness: sharingculture.ca

Glooscap Heritage Centre: glooscapheritagecentre.com

Leonard Paul (Mi'kmaw painter): leonardpaul.com

Mi'kmaq Association for Cultural Studies: mikmaq-assoc.ca

Mi'kmaq–Maliseet Nations News: mmnn.ca

Mi'kmaw Native Friendship Centre: mymnfc.com

Mi'kmaw Resource Centre, Cape Breton University: cbu.ca/mrc/mikmaq-first-nations

L'nu'k: The People

Native Council of Nova Scotia: ncns.ca

Stone Bear Tracks and Trails (Mi'kmaw nature retreat): stonebear.ca

Author's tip: Google "powwow trails" to learn when and where powwows are scheduled throughout Mi'kma'ki.

Places to Visit

Membertou Heritage Park

> Membertou First Nation, Sydney, Cape Breton

Mi'kmaq Heritage and Cultural Centre

> Millbrook First Nation, Truro

Mother Earth Lodge

> Metepenagiag First Nation, Red Bank, New Brunswick

Nature Trails

> Lennox Island First Nation, Prince Edward Island

Index

Numbers set in italics refer to images

L'nu'k: The People

L'nu'k: The People

Other books in the Compass: True Stories for Kids Series

Children of the Titanic
ISBN: 978-1-55109-892-0

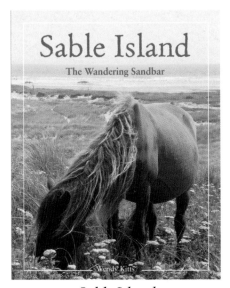

Sable Island
ISBN: 978-1-55109-865-4

Birchtown
ISBN: 978-1-77108-166-5

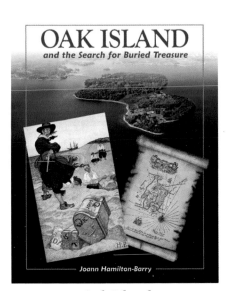

Oak Island
ISBN: 978-1-77108-342-3